# Frederick Noad's
# CLASSICAL GUITAR TREASURY

Duets & Ensembles

Compiled, edited and
fingered by Frederick Noad

**Chester Music**
(A division of Music Sales Limited)
8/9 Frith Street, London W1V 5TZ

# Introduction

The arrangements and transcriptions collected in this volume comprise
a number of works previously published in the Noad Guitar Library series.
Some, such as the duets by Dowland, are well-known works but others,
including the J. B. Marella duets are less well-known and deserve wider recognition.
Their striking charm was first brought to public attention on the wonderful
recordings of the duet team of Ida Presti and Alexandre Lagoya.

The collection from Praetorius for an ensemble of four guitars serves as
easily readable material for those who gather together to play, for instance in
guitar societies. Praetorius had an ear for a good tune, and his arrangements
derived from some of the most popular tunes of his day. Also great fun to play is
L'Encouragement for two guitars by Sor, arguably his best duet. One extended work
for flute or violin and guitar is included, the Grand Duo Concertante of Mauro Giuliani.
Representing one of the finest works in the repertoire for this combination,
this work has been recorded by a number of leading artists.

In terms of period the pieces span from the late Renaissance to the early
19th century. With the exception of the Handel keyboard originals, most of the
pieces were written for plucked stringed instruments, including the Renaissance
lute, baroque guitar and lute and the six stringed guitar of the classical period.

In fact the common element in this diverse collection is perhaps to be found
in the strong melodic quality of the works, which has been a major factor in their
selection. I hope that guitarists will find something old and something new to
entertain them in this volume!

Frederick Noad

Exclusive distributors:
Music Sales Limited, Newmarket Road, Bury St. Edmunds, Suffolk IP33 3YB.

This book © Copyright 1998 Chester Music.
Order No. CH61467
ISBN 0-7119-6978-7

Cover by Michael Bell Design.
Cover image courtesy of The National Gallery.
Printed in Great Britain by Redwood Books, Trowbridge, Wiltshire

# Contents

*(All works for guitar duet unless otherwise indicated)*

# John Dowland

John Dowland (1563-1626) has been described as 'the rarest Musician that his age did behold.' A celebrated performer as well as composer, Dowland travelled extensively in Europe, and served as Lutenist to Christian IV of Denmark at a time when, possibly by reason of his religious beliefs, he was unable to obtain a post under Queen Elizabeth. Finally in 1612 he was appointed one of the King's lutes at the court of James I, a very belated recognition of a man who was by then considered the finest lutenist in Europe.

The present edition is prepared primarily for guitarists, who more than any will be the performers of this music. The fingering offered is for standard guitar tuning, but more experienced players may prefer to tune the third string down a semitone to F sharp. This parallels the intervals of the lute and greatly simplifies the playing of some passages.

# My Lord Willoughby's Welcome Home

John Dowland (1563-1626)
Transcribed, edited and fingered by Frederick Noad

# My Lord Chamberlain, His Galliard

John Dowland (1563-1626)

Transcribed, edited and fingered by Frederick Noad

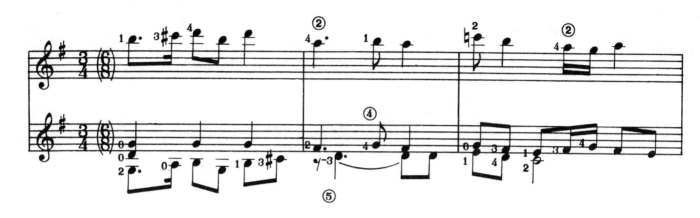

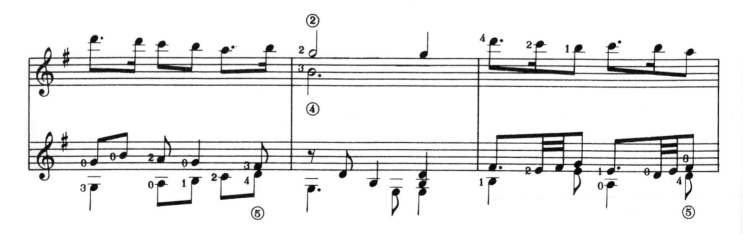

These transcriptions are drawn from the ballet music to Alcina. Handel did not, as far as is known, write for the lute or guitar, although he did occasionally use the theorbo-lute as an accompanying instrument. Nevertheless the simpler pieces have great charm when played on guitar, and the transcriptions give students the opportunity for acquaintance with one of the greatest of all musicians.

# Menuet

George Frederic Handel (1685-1759)

Transcribed for guitar by Frederick Noad

# Musette

George Frederic Handel (1685-1759)
Transcribed for guitar by Frederick Noad

# J.B. Marella

The duets of J.B. Marella were first brought to public attention in this century by the celebrated guitarists Ida Presti and Alexandre Lagoya. The source of these duets was a book published in 1762 entitled *Compositions for the Cetra or Guittar with an Accompaniment,* a copy of which is to be found in the library of the British Museum. Of the composer almost nothing is known apart from the fact that he composed two works for violin and basso continuo, the first published in Dublin in 1753 and the second in London in 1757. At the time of publication of the present collection he was resident in London in Great Poultney Street. The dedications of the two London publications to the Countess of Pembroke and Lady Mary Grey imply access to aristocratic circles, and it is reasonable to suppose that Marella was one of the Italian music-masters so much in vogue at the time.

Whether the music was intended for the guitar proper is at least open to question. The fashionable instrument of the time was a modernised form of the 16th century cittern also known as the Cetra or English guitar. It had metal strings, normally four paired and two single, and was tuned to major triads, most usually in the key of C. So it is possible that *Compositions for the Cetra or Guittar* did not offer an alternative but simply gave two common names of the same instrument. Further evidence of this appears in the dedication where Marella writes 'I believe it will not, in the present Age, be thought necessary for me to say anything in favour of the Instrument for which these Pieces were chiefly designed.' Later he adds 'And, should the Compositions I now lay before your Ladyship conduce to the general Improvement of the Guittar, I shall think my endeavours sufficiently rewarded.'

Most of the pieces in the collection are in the key of A major, necessitating the A tuning of the cittern but also placing them conveniently within the range of the five-course guitar of the period. The upper parts contain the numerous successions of thirds typical of cittern music of the period. The instrumentation of the basso continuo is not specified, but the writing of the bass in the treble clef implies the use of a second plucked instrument.

The arrangements presented here have been adapted to the modern guitar. The thirds which were so easy to play on the cittern by virtue of its tuning have in some cases been divided between the two guitars for greater ease, and in the lower part the sixth string has been used occasionally when the want of it was apparent from the bass line.

Whatever the original intention may have been, the pieces make excellent guitar duets, offering the flavour of a period usually neglected by guitarists.

# Giga

J.B. Marella

Edited, fingered and transcribed by Frederick Noad

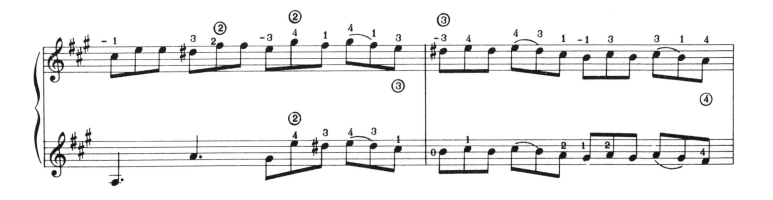

16

# March

J.B. Marella
Edited, fingered and transcribed by Frederick Noad

19

# Opertura

J.B. Marella
Edited, fingered and transcribed by Frederick Noad

Andantino

Guitar Duet

# Minuetto

J.B. Marella
Edited, fingered and transcribed by Frederick Noad

# Andante

J.B. Marella
Edited, fingered and transcribed by Frederick Noad

27

28

# Minuetto

J.B. Marella
Edited, fingered and transcribed by Frederick Noad

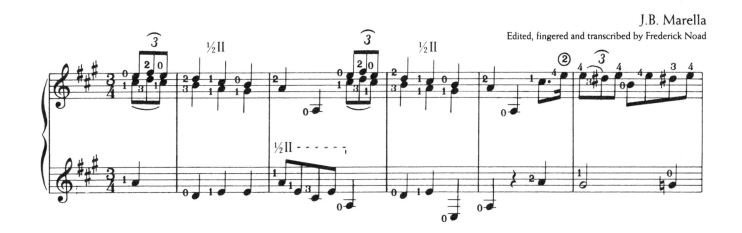

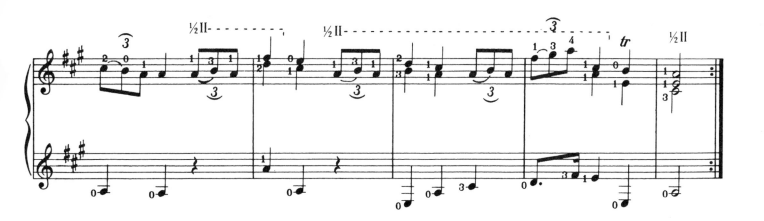

# Siciliana

J.B. Marella
Edited, fingered and transcribed by Frederick Noad

# Andantino

J.B. Marella
Edited, fingered and transcribed by Frederick Noad

# Allegro Maestoso

J.B. Marella
Edited, fingered and transcribed by Frederick Noad

# Andantino

J.B. Marella
Edited, fingered and transcribed by Frederick Noad

47

## Guitar Duet

# Minuetto

J.B. Marella
Edited, fingered and transcribed by Frederick Noad

# Fernando Sor

Fernando Sor (1778-1839) may be considered the most distinguished composer for the guitar of the 19th century, as well as one of its most successful performers. Formally trained in the school of music of the Montserrat monastery, Sor's first major work was an opera, *Telemacco*, which was presented in Barcelona when he was only seventeen years old. A number of compositions followed, and Sor enjoyed the patronage of such prominent figures as the Duchess of Alba and the Duke of Medinacelli; but no guitar works are known to have been published prior to Sor's departure from Spain for Paris at about the age of thirty-five.

Paris was at the time a centre of guitar interest, with considerable amateur and dilettante enthusiasm stimulated by teachers and performers such as Antoine Lemoine, Antoine Messonier and in particular the Italian, Ferdinando Carulli. This interest generated a lively market for guitar music, especially easy pieces accessible to the amateur. In London, interest in the guitar was also strong and created a demand for new publications. Sor's first works for the guitar were published in both London and Paris, and consisted of easy 'Divertimentos' likely to appeal to the amateur. Later his friend and publisher Antoine Messonier co-ordinated his work into a major edition with opus numbers, and his compositions reflect a greater freedom of expression with more technical demands from the player than the early works for amateurs.

*L'Encouragement* Op.34 appeared in 1828 and was the first duet published by Sor. It was probably intended for use with his students, since in its original form the first guitar had all the melodic parts, while the second guitar was relegated to the subsidiary role of accompanist. In a later version edited and published by Napoleon Coste the parts were redistributed so as to give both players a turn at the melodies, and it is this version that is printed below. The fingering is editorial, and should be regarded as a suggestion only.

# L'Encouragement Op.34

Fernando Sor (1778-1839)
Edited and fingered by Frederick Noad

THEME

Andantino

**VARIATION I**

## VARIATION II
Mineur

VARIATION III

VALSE

# Ferdinando Carulli

The Neapolitan Ferdinando Carulli (1770-1841) was one of the most successful and celebrated early masters of the guitar at a time when the instrument, with its recently added sixth string, was becoming immensely popular among the amateur public. The role of the guitar had been principally one of accompaniment, but in the first years of the 19th century the solo possibilities were being explored by a handful of pioneering performers, Carulli among them, and the public responded enthusiastically by abandoning its former allegiance to the cittern, the favoured 'dilettante' instrument of the previous half century.

In response to popular demand, a flood of publications poured onto the markets of Paris, Vienna and other major cities; and Carulli alone produced more than 400 works in a period of twelve years. By 1808 he was established in Paris and his work was in demand by the leading publishers. His compositions included duets, trios, works for guitar and piano and even a number of Concerti for guitar and orchestra. His *Method for the Guitar*, Op.241, was published in 1810, and has been constantly reprinted.

This duet was published before the *Method*, probably in 1809, and bore the title *Grandes Variations Pour Deux Guitares Sur la Marche de l'Opera d'Aline, Musique de H. Berton, Composées par Ferdinando Carulli*, Op.219. Henri Berton (1767-1844) composed the opera *Aline* in 1803. In an age when no means of sound recording existed, operatic variations, fantasies etc. on popular themes served a purpose similar to that of the record - enabling the public to play their favourites at home. As a result, the guitar literature of the time is full of such memories of operas now long forgotten.

The parts in this duet are balanced so that the second guitar is not relegated to the role of mere accompanist. The more dazzling variations should be played up to tempo to achieve the intended 'virtuoso' sparkle.

The form of notation is that of the early days of the guitar, when the length of bass notes is not spelled out as a separate part. However, the intention of the composer is so obvious, in spite of the less efficient notation, that it seems preferable to present the work as it was originally. Fingering has been added where necessary; all dynamic and tempo markings are those of the original edition.

# Grand Variations for Two Guitars

from the Opera *'Aline'* Op.219

Ferdinando Carulli (1770-1841)
Revised and edited by Frederick Noad

# Introduction

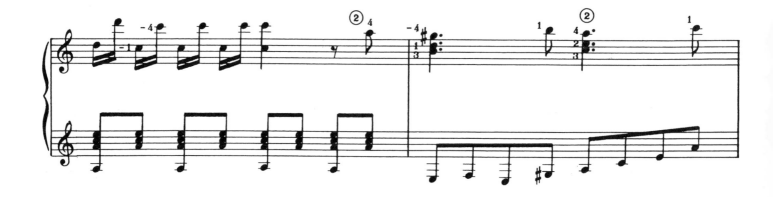

# March

# Variation I

# Variation II

D. C. al Fine

# Variation III

# Variation IV

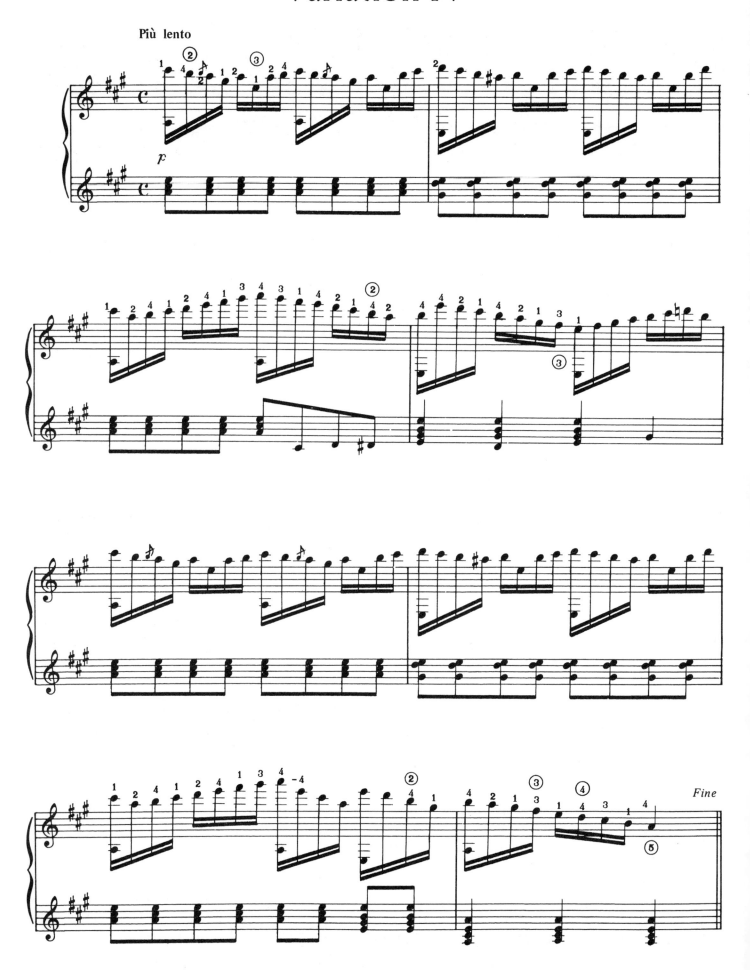

D. C. al Fine

# Variation V

D. C. al Fine

89

# Variation VI

D. C. al Fine

91

# Variation VII

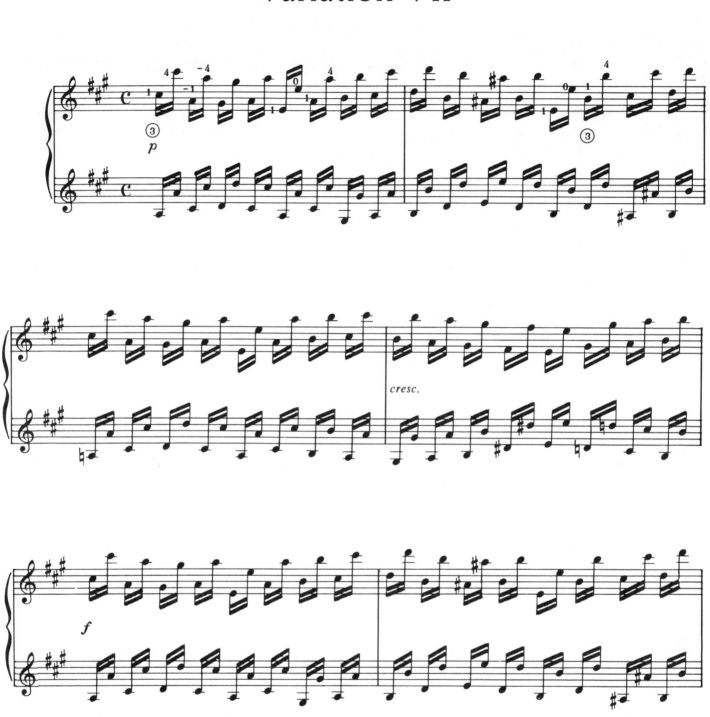

D. C. al Fine

93

# Variation VIII

# Variation IX

# Allegretto

# Mauro Giuliani

Of the many works by Giuliani for flute or violin and guitar this is one of the most satisfying
for both instrumentalists, as the guitarist is not relegated to the role of accompanist, as in the majority of
such works of the period, but truly shares the duet role.

This edition is based on the original Artaria publication of 1817 (pl. nr. 2501).
The two separate parts have been amalgamated into a score, since many players
seem to prefer this, and a suggested fingering has been added to the guitar part.

# Grand Duo Concertante, Op.85

Mauro Giuliani
Edited and fingered by Frederick Noad

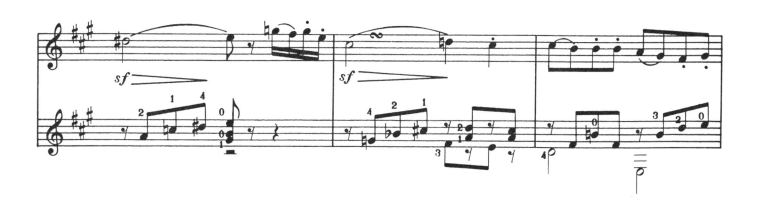

106

SCHERZO
Vivace

TRIO

D.C. scherzo

Allegretto espressivo

124

126

127

134

135

# Michael Praetorius

## Dances of the Late Renaissance from *Terpsichore*

The *Terpsichore* collection of dances - the greatest of its time - was compiled by Michael Praetorius (a latinized version of the name Schultz) on a commission from Duke Friedrich Ulrich who had acquired the melodies from his French dancing master. The task of Praetorius was to compose extra parts, thereby making the music suitable for the instrumental ensembles of the time. He was assisted in this work by Francisque Caroubel, and the latter's contributions are identified by the initials F.C. Praetorius' own arrangements are identified by the initials M.P.C. except in cases where he added only inner parts, identifying the latter with the word *incerti* (anonymous).

Although the melodies were published as 'French' dances it is evident that some popular tunes of other origin had found their way into the dancing master's repertoire. For instance No.1 has the melody of *Mistress Winter's Jump* by John Dowland and No.7 is a setting of the air *I Care Not For These Ladies* by Thomas Campion published in Phillip Rosseter's *Book of Ayres* in 1601. However, these are the exceptions rather than the rule, the predominant flavour being that of country dances.

The dances are suitable for many combinations of instruments, and sound well on guitars. The upper parts are high enough to provide reading practice in the higher positions of the fingerboard, and less expert players will find little difficulty in the middle parts. In the five-part arrangements the third voice has been combined with the bass to enable four players to cover all parts. However, if a fifth player is present, this bass part may be divided into two for greater ease.

Dances of the Late Renaissance from *Terpsichore*

# Gaillarde I

300 Incerti
Edited and fingered by Frederick Noad

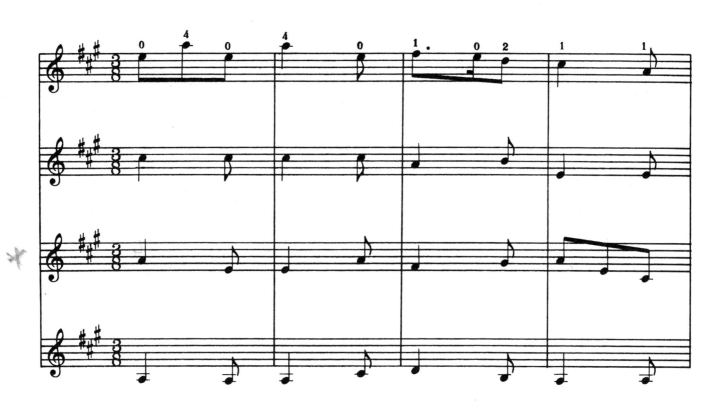

# Gaillarde II

292 M.P.C.
Edited and fingered by Frederick Noad

FEB 2018

141

# Gaillarde III

284 F.C.
Edited and fingered by Frederick Noad

MAR 6/2018

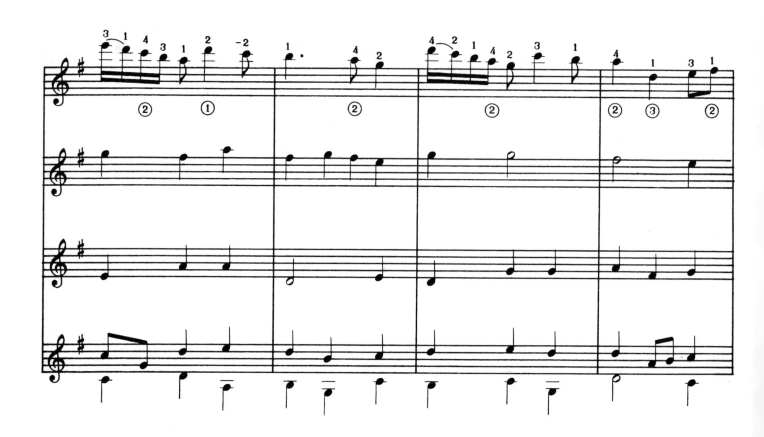

# Gaillarde IV

*296 Incerti*
Edited and fingered by Frederick Noad

# Bransle Double

12 M.P.C.
Edited and fingered by Frederick Noad

# Pavane de Spaigne

29 F.C.
Edited and fingered by Frederick Noad

# Courante I

158 M.P.C.

Edited and fingered by Frederick Noad

# Courante II

179 M.P.C.

Edited and fingered by Frederick Noad

# Spagnoletta

28 M.P.C.
Edited and fingered by Frederick Noad

158

# Volte I

223 F.C.
Edited and fingered by Frederick Noad

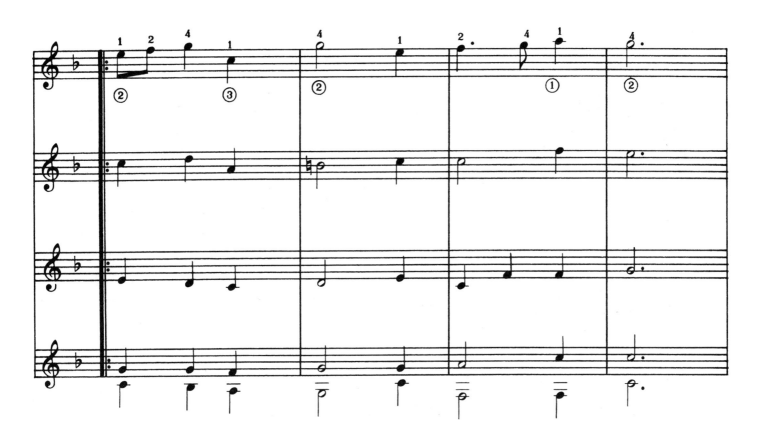

# Volte II

210 M.P.C.
Edited and fingered by Frederick Noad

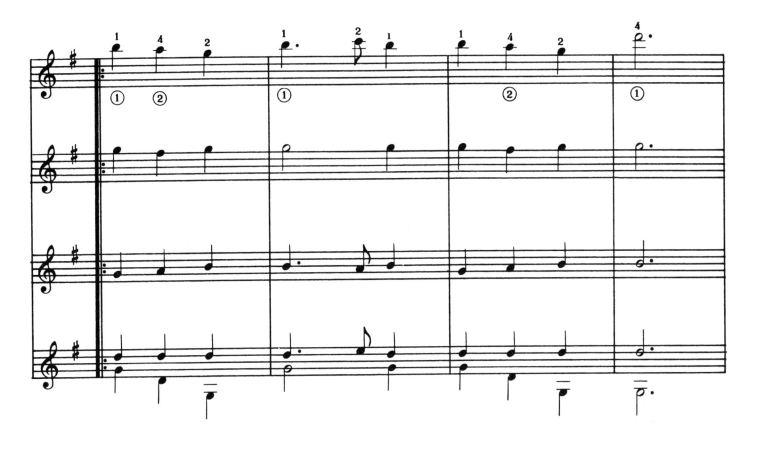

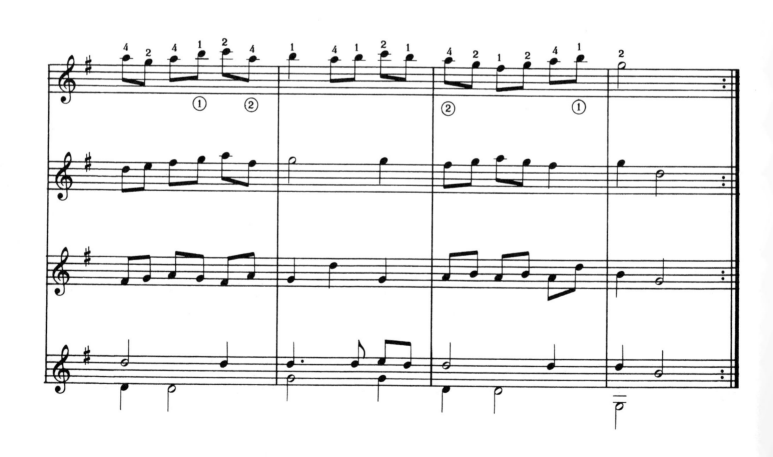